The Black Belt ABC's

Written & Illustrated by Melissa La Cour

Dedicated to all the students, past and present at Pace Karate Vernon. You'll never know the impact you've had on me.

Meet Omelette!
He is a new student at Eggcellent Martial Arts hoping to someday earn his black belt. Along his journey he will also be learning the Black Belt ABC's. Let's learn this alphabet of positive traits along with him...

Yet they know the importance of keeping life in balance.

Black belts are courageous...

They have *exceptional* skill thanks to their years of martial arts training.

They are *genuine* and *gracious* towards others.

Black belts have humble spirits.

They keep *integrity* and strive
to make a positive impact.

Black belts are joyful!

They are kind.

They are
loving.

Those who have achieved the rank are *motivated* leaders.

Black belts have a *noble* character.

They are *optimistic* in any circumstance.

Black belts persevere through hardships.

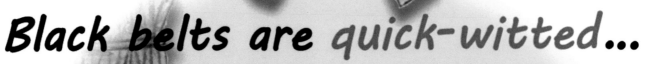

Black belts are quick-witted...

Black belts are *self-reliant* because they do not let obstacles stand in their way.

Black belts are trusted in their circle.

Black belts are unique characters.

They are *versatile* individuals.

Black belts have grown *wise* from their years of training.

A black belt's x-factor helps them stand out from the crowd.

Black belts know their why, their purpose.